Investigative Maths

Developing children's investigative and thinking skills in the Daily Maths Lesson

Year 3

Peter Clarke

William Collins' dream of knowledge for all began with the publication of his first book in 1819. A self-educated mill worker, he not only enriched millions of lives, but also founded a flourishing publishing house. Today, staying true to this spirit, Collins books are packed with inspiration, innovation and practical expertise. They place you at the centre of a world of possibility and give you exactly what you need to explore it.

Collins. Do more.

Published by Collins
An imprint of HarperCollins*Publishers*
77–85 Fulham Palace Road
Hammersmith
London
W6 8JB

Browse the complete Collins catalogue at
www.collinseducation.com

10 9 8 7 6 5 4 3 2 1

ISBN 0 00 719473 0

Peter Clarke asserts his moral right to be identified as the author of this work

British Library Cataloguing in Publication Data
A Catalogue record for this publication is available from the British Library

Publishing Manager: Melanie Hoffman
Project Editor: Natasha Reid
Editor: Jean Rustean
Cover design by Susi Martin
Cover illustration by Gary Dunn
Series design by Neil Adams
Illustrations by Juliet Breese

Printed and bound by Martins the Printers, Berwick on Tweed

Contents

Introduction

Mathematical problem solving encompasses both using and applying mathematics to the solution of problems arising from the environment and reasoning and investigating questions that have arisen from within mathematics itself.

Being able to use mathematics to analyse situations and solve real-life problems is a major reason for studying the subject. Frequent use of everyday experiences will give meaning to the children's mathematical experiences. Children need to be able to apply the mathematics they have learned to real-life situations in their environment. They also need to be able to interpret and make meaning from their results. Teachers should structure situations in which children investigate problems relevant to their daily lives and relating to the recent mathematical knowledge, skills and understanding the children have acquired.

Studies of effective teachers of numeracy (Askew *et al.* 1997) have found that the most effective teachers have a 'connectionist' orientation to the teaching of mathematics. These teachers encourage children to think and talk about what they are doing and to make connections between different areas and aspects of the subject.

Investigative Maths is a series of six books for Year 1 to Year 6. It is designed to assist children to practise and consolidate the three strands of the Mathematics National Curriculum Attainment Target 1 – Using and applying mathematics: problem solving, communicating and reasoning; as well as the problem solving strand of the National Numeracy Strategy (NNS) *Framework for teaching mathematics R – 6*. At the same time other key mathematical strands are also developed such as numbers and the number system, calculations, and measures, shape and space.

Investigative Maths aims to provide teachers with a resource that enables children to:

- use and apply mathematics to solve problems arising from the environment
- reason and investigate questions that have arisen from within mathematics itself
- practise their pure mathematical knowledge and skills in an applied context
- apply their mathematical problem solving skills in contexts that are topical, relevant and meaningful

The activities

Investigative Maths contains two different types of activities:

Everyday problem solving

These activities include problems arising from the environment.

The activities in this section have been organised into themes. There are 12 themes, each with four different activities. The four activities can either be used together in one lesson, with different groups working on different activities, or individually over the course of a week or more.

When children solve everyday problems:

- the purpose and meaning is clear
- it is motivating

- it allows them to take control of the mathematics, choosing methods that suit them
- they are likely to feel confident about multi-tasking
- the context provides many clues and stimuli to support their thinking
- the mathematics is practical rather than abstract, and builds more obviously on children's previous experiences

Mathematical problem solving

These activities include problems arising from within mathematics itself.

When children solve mathematical problems they:

- use prior mathematical knowledge to acquire new mathematical knowledge
- make connections

Resources

- Almost all the activities in *Investigative Maths* suggest that pencil and paper be given to the children. This allows the children to feel free to work out the answers and record their thinking in ways that are appropriate to them. Giving children a large sheet of paper, such as A1, provides them with an excellent prompt to use when discussing their work, especially during the plenary. It also aids assessment for children's problem solving, communicating and reasoning skills.
- An important problem solving skill is to be able to identify not only the mathematics, but also what equipment to use. For this reason many of the activities do not name the specific resources that are needed. For example, in problems involving measures, the resources section states simply 'measuring equipment' to make teachers aware that a range of measuring equipment will need to be on hand for the children to choose.
- Teachers also need to be aware that some of the activities require them or the children to bring in to school resources from home.

Answers

- In the *Mathematical problem solving* section, answers are given to the primary activities where necessary, not to the extensions .
- In the *Everyday problem solving* section, no answers are given.

Investigative Maths and the daily mathematics lesson

The activities contained in *Investigative Maths* are ideally suited to the daily mathematics lesson. They can be used to:

- introduce new mathematical concepts using a discovery approach to teaching and learning
- consolidate children's understanding of previously taught mathematical concepts
- provide an opportunity for children to use and apply their 'pure' mathematical knowledge in more applied, problem solving and investigative contexts
- extend the more able pupils
- challenge the 'quick finishers'

Although the activities are designed to be used by individuals, pairs or groups of children, they will be enhanced greatly if children are able to work together in pairs or groups. By working collaboratively, children are more likely to develop their problem solving, communicating and reasoning skills.

Problem solving skills

Investigative Maths aims to develop in children the key skills required to tackle and solve mathematical investigations.

These include:
- reading and making sense of a problem
- recognising key words, relevant information and redundant information
- finding parts of a problem that can be tackled
- recognising the mathematics which can be used to help solve a problem
- deciding which number operation(s) to perform and in which order
- choosing an efficient way of calculating
- presenting information and results in a clear and organised way
- changing measurements to the same units before calculating
- getting into the habit of checking for themselves whether the answer makes sense

Thinking skills

The National Curriculum (2000) outlines the thinking skills that complement the key knowledge, skills and understanding which are embedded in the primary curriculum.

Investigative Maths aims to develop in children these key thinking skills.

Information – processing skills
- locate, collect relevant information
- sort, classify, sequence, compare and analyse part and/or whole relationships

Reasoning skills
- give reasons for opinions and actions
- draw inferences and make deductions
- use precise language to explain what they think
- make judgements and decisions informed by reason or evidence

Enquiry skills
- ask relevant questions
- pose and define problems
- plan what to do and how to research
- predict outcomes and anticipate conclusions
- test conclusions and improve ideas

Creative thinking skills
- generate and extend ideas
- suggest hypotheses
- apply imagination
- look for alternative innovative outcomes

Evaluative skills

- evaluate information
- judge the value of what they read, hear or do
- develop criteria for judging the value of their own and others' work or ideas
- have confidence in their judgement

Problem solving strategies

If children are actively to engage in mathematical investigations they must be taught appropriate problem solving strategies.

Children need to be taught to:
- look for a pattern or sequence
- experiment or act out a problem
- make a drawing or model
- make a list, table or chart
- write a number sentence
- see mathematical connections
- make and test a prediction
- make a generalisation
- establish a proof
- account for all known possibilities
- solve a simpler related problem
- work backwards

A model for mathematical investigations

To be successful at solving mathematical investigations, children need to:
- be given ample opportunities to practise problem solving skills and strategies
- work systematically and co-operatively
- use what knowledge and skills they have to help acquire new knowledge and skills
- develop self monitoring and self assessment
- talk about their work and reflect on their thinking

The model on page 8 provides children with a systematic approach to solving mathematical investigations. It also enables children to practise and develop their thinking skills.

Photocopy and enlarge this page, make it into a poster, and display it for all the class to see and follow.

Children need to be taught to use this model flexibly. They must realise that:
- not all eight stages of the model are required for every investigation
- the amount of time that is spent on each of the eight stages depends upon the nature of the investigation
- any stage in the model can be revisited at any time

A model for mathematical investigations

Recognise
What is the problem?

Reflect
What have I learned from this?

Use
What do I already know that can help me solve this problem?

Share
Let's tell others.

Support
What do I need to find out and use to help me solve this problem?

Check and assess
- Am I correct?
- How well did I do?

Decide and try
- How might I go about solving this problem?
- What is the best way?
- Let's try.

Review
Is it working?
Yes – Let's continue.
No – Let's go back.

Investigative Maths (Y3) © HarperCollins*Publishers* Ltd 2005

Curriculum information

The activities in *Investigative Maths* are designed to improve children's attainment in the three strands of the National Curriculum Attainment Target 1 – Using and applying mathematics.

In *problem solving* by:

- using a range of problem solving strategies
- trying different approaches to a problem
- applying mathematics in a new context
- checking their results

In *communicating* by:

- interpreting information
- recording information systematically
- using mathematical language, symbols, notation and diagrams correctly and precisely
- presenting and interpreting methods, solutions and conclusions in the context of the problem

In *reasoning* by:

- giving clear explanations of their methods and reasoning
- investigating and making general statements
- recognising patterns in their results
- making use of a wider range of evidence to justify results through logical reasoned argument
- drawing their own conclusions

The activities also provide children with an opportunity to practise and consolidate the following Year 3 solving problems objectives from the NNS *Framework*:

Topic: *Making decisions*

- Choose and use appropriate operations (including multiplication and division) to solve word problems, and appropriate ways of calculating: mental, mental with jottings, pencil and paper.

Topic: *Reasoning about numbers or shapes*

- Solve mathematical problems or puzzles, recognise simple patterns and relationships, generalise and predict. Suggest extensions by asking 'What if...?'
- Investigate a general statement about familiar numbers or shapes by finding examples that satisfy it.
- Explain methods and reasoning orally and, where appropriate, in writing.

Topic: *Problems involving 'real life', money or measures*

- Solve word problems involving numbers in 'real life', money and measures, using one or more steps, including finding totals and giving change, and working out which coins to pay.
- Explain how the problem was solved.

In addition to these objectives, the charts on pages 10 and 11 show which other strand(s) and topic(s) each of the activities covers.

Everyday problem solving

These activities include problems arising from the environment.

Page	Activity	Theme	Title	Counting, properties of numbers and number sequences	Place value and ordering	Estimating and rounding	Fractions	Addition	Subtraction	Multiplication	Division	Money	Organising and using data	Measures: Length (L), Mass (M), Capacity (C), Time (T)	Shape and space
			Strand	Numbers and the number system				Calculations				Solving problems		Measures, shape and space	
14	1a	Football	Half-time scores	●											
14	1b		Football results					●	●				●		
15	1c		Football club			●		●		●		●			
15	1d		School pitch											●L	
16	2a	Letters	Envelopes											●L	●
16	2b		Give me the dates	●										●T	
17	2c		Home school directions											●L,T	●
17	2d		How much to post?									●			
18	3a	Fitness	Workout											●T	
18	3b		In a minute						●	●				●T	
19	3c		How fit?										●	●T	
19	3d		An hour a day					●	●				●	●T	
20	4a	Tangrams	Investigating tangrams												●
20	4b		Tangram shapes												●
21	4c		Tangram animals												●
21	4d		Design your own tangram											●L	●
22	5a	Dice	2 dice totals					●					●		
22	5b		Greatest total					●	●	●	●		●		
23	5c		Total dots	●				●							
23	5d		Make a die											●L	●
24	6a	Television	Right angle programmes												●
24	6b		How much television?			●		●						●T	
25	6c		Favourite programme										●		
25	6d		Pay TV					●		●		●			
26	7a	Codes	Pattern code	●	●								●		
26	7b		Wheel code	●	●								●		
27	7c		Binary code	●	●			●					●		
27	7d		Make your own code	●	●								●		
28	8a	School meals	Planning a school menu									●	●		
28	8b		Left over food											●M	
29	8c		Value for money									●			
29	8d		Popular dinners										●		
30	9a	Traffic and transport	School road	●		●	●						●	●T	
30	9b		Traffic lights	●									●	●T	
31	9c		Public transport			●						●	●	●T	
31	9d		Cost of public transport									●	●	●T	
32	10a	Relations	Happy Birthday Daphne	●				●	●					●T	
32	10b		Living relations	●				●	●					●T	
33	10c		Could your relations...?											●T	
33	10d		Brothers and sisters										●		
34	11a	Newspapers	How many papers?					●	●	●	●	●	●		
34	11b		Fractions of a newspaper			●		●	●	●	●				
35	11c		Numbers in papers	●											
35	11d		The value of newspapers										●	●M	
36	12a	Clothes	Clothing weights					●						●M	
36	12b		Tailor made	●		●								●L	●
37	12c		Clothe yourself					●		●		●			
37	12d		New school uniform	●				●		●		●			

Mathematical problem solving

These activities include problems arising from within mathematics itself.

Page	Activity	Title	Counting, properties of numbers and number sequences	Place value and ordering	Estimating and rounding	Fractions	Addition	Subtraction	Multiplication	Division	Money	Organising and using data	Measures: Length (L), Mass (M), Capacity (C), Time (T)	Shape and space
38	13	Odd and even 3-digit numbers	●											
38	14	Number sequences	●											
39	15	Seeing patterns	●											
39	16	Numbers between…		●								●		
40	17	1, 10 and 100		●										
40	18	Rounding			●							●		
41	19	Pages, lines and words			●									
41	20	Fractions that total 1				●						●		
42	21	Buying sweets				●						●		
42	22	Equivalent fractions				●						●		
43	23	Fractions of numbers				●								
43	24	60 and 100			●		●	●						
44	25	Pairs of 2-digit numbers					●					●		
44	26	Multiples of 10					●					●		
45	27	Smaller from the larger						●				●		
45	28	Calendar calculations					●	●				●	●T	
46	29	Choose 3 numbers					●	●				●		
46	30	Making numbers					●	●				●		
47	31	10 card calculations					●	●				●		
47	32	All 2s and 5s					●	●						
48	33	409					●	●						
48	34	Making palindromic numbers					●	●				●		
49	35	Date of birth			●		●	●				●		
49	36	Odd and even calculations	●				●	●				●		
50	37	Which signs?					●	●						
50	38	Multiplying by 10 and 100		●					●					
51	39	Double multiplications							●					
51	40	Halving chains								●		●		
52	41	Dividing by 10 and 100		●						●				
52	42	Remainder of 1								●		●		
53	43	More remainders								●		●		
53	44	Special squares							●	●				
54	45	Multiplications and divisions							●	●				
54	46	× ÷ 10 000		●					●	●				
55	47	Making 24					●	●	●	●		●		
55	48	Toy cars					●	●			●	●		
56	49	1 note and 3 coins					●	●			●	●		
56	50	Receiving change					●	●			●	●		
57	51	Measuring with ropes					●	●				●	●L	
57	52	50 g, 100 g, 500 g					●	●				●	●M	
58	53	Filling buckets				●	●					●	●C	
58	54	This year	●									●	●T	
59	55	Weekend	●									●	●T	
59	56	Decking							●			●		●
60	57	Symmetrical flags										●		●
60	58	Right angle shapes												●
61	59	Ronnie the Robot										●		●
61	60	Tessellating shapes												●

Assessment and record keeping

Investigative Maths activities may be used with the whole class or with groups of children as an assessment activity. Linked to the topic that is being studied at present, *Investigative Maths* will provide you with an indication of how well the children have understood the objectives being covered as well as their problem solving skills.

The Assessment and record keeping format on page 13 can be used to assess and level children in Attainment Target 1: Using and applying mathematics. By observing individual children while they undertake an *Investigative Maths* activity, discussing their work with them, and subsequently marking their work, you will be able to gain a good understanding of their problem solving, communicating and reasoning skills.

Your judgements about an individual child's abilities should also take into account:

- mastery of other objectives from the 'Solving problems' strand of the NNS *Framework*
- performance in whole class discussions
- participation in group work
- work presented in exercise books
- any other written evidence

Once you have decided which level 'best fits' a particular child write the child's name in the box under the appropriate level. You may wish to identify how competent a child is at that level by using the following key:

C – Becoming competent in most criteria at this level

B – Competent in most criteria at this level

A – Very competent in most criteria at this level

It is envisaged that one copy of the Assessment and record keeping format would be used for your entire class.

Attainment Target 1: Using and applying mathematics
Assessment and record keeping format

Year: _____ Class: _____

Teacher: _____

LEVEL 2

Problem solving
- Select and use material in some classroom activities.
- Select and use mathematics for some classroom activities.
- Begin to develop own strategies for solving a problem.
- Begin to understand ways of working through a problem.

Communicating
- Discuss work using mathematical language.
- Respond to and ask mathematical questions.
- Begin to represent work using symbols and simple diagrams.
- Explain why an answer is correct.

Reasoning
- Ask questions such as: 'What would happen if…?' 'Why?'.
- Begin to develop simple strategies.

LEVEL 3

Problem solving
- Develop different mathematical approaches to a problem.
- Look for ways to overcome difficulties.
- Begin to make decisions and realise that results may vary according to the 'rule' used.
- Begin to organise work.
- Check results.

Communicating
- Discuss mathematical work.
- Begin to explain thinking.
- Use and interpret mathematical symbols and diagrams.

Reasoning
- Understand a general statement.
- Investigate general statements and predictions by finding and trying out examples.

LEVEL 4

Problem solving
- Develop own strategies for solving problems.
- Use own strategies for working within mathematics.
- Use own strategies for applying mathematics to practical contexts.

Communicating
- Present information and results in a clear and organised way.

Reasoning
- Search for solutions by trying out own ideas.

GENERAL COMMENTS

• pencil and paper

1a Half-time scores

- At the end of the United v Wanderers match the score was 3–3.
- What could the half-time scores have been?

- What if the full-time score was 10–10?
- What about a score of 5–4 at full-time?
- Make a rule for working out how many different half-time scores there are using just the final score.

1b Football results

- Look at the football results.
- Write about things you notice.

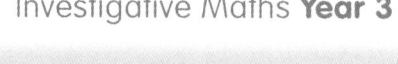

- newspaper showing football results
- pencil and paper

- Think about:
  - Are football teams more likely to win at home or away?
  - Is there a difference in the scores in each division? Do teams in the First Division score more than teams in the Fourth division?
  - Is there a relationship between goals for and goals against?
  - Does attendance depend on the positioning in the league table?

- pencil and paper

1c Football club

- Thinking about either your local football club or your favourite football club, work out approximately how much money the club takes each game.

- Think about:
  - how much a ticket costs
  - different priced tickets
  - how many seats the stadium holds.

- squared paper
- ruler
- pencil

1d School pitch

- What is the size of your school football pitch?
- Draw a plan of your school pitch to scale.
  Don't forget to mark in the half-way line and goal areas.

- How does the size of your school football pitch compare to that of a professional football pitch? How much smaller / bigger is it?

2a Envelopes

- sheet of A4 paper
- scissors
- glue
- sticky tape
- ruler
- pencil and paper

- Design and make the largest envelope you can from a sheet of A4 paper.
- Write instructions as to how you made your envelope so that someone else can make exactly the same envelope.

- Without seeing the envelope that a friend made, can you make their envelope using their instructions?

2b Give me the dates

- pencil and paper

- Work out the date and the day of the week for each of the events in the letter.

7 Rue Saint Vincent
Nice 06300
France

Tuesday 4th August

Dear Aunty Jean,
Thank you for the ball you gave me for my birthday last Saturday. We arrived in Nice 2 days ago. The weather is great. Yesterday and today we went to the beach. If it is sunny tomorrow mum said we can go on a picnic. A week tomorrow we are going to the mountains for 10 days. The day after we arrive there my friend Michael and his parents arrive. He is 12 years old and really wicked. He is 4 years older than me but his birthday is on the same day as mine. When we leave there we are going back to Nice for 3 days then back home, but I don't have to go back to school for another 7 days after that.

Love from
Peter

- Write a letter similar to that above for a friend to work out the dates and the days of the week.

2c Home school directions

- squared
  paper
- coloured
  pencils
- pencil

- Imagine writing a letter to a pen pal
  in Australia. Your pen pal is coming
  to visit you and when they
  arrive at your home they
  will need directions on how
  to get from your home to
  your school so that they
  can meet you.

- Write out the directions
  and draw a simple map.

- In your letter don't forget to tell them:
  - how long the journey will take
  - the approximate distance of each part of the journey.

2d How much to post?

- Post Office
  Price Guide
- pencil and
  paper

- Imagine a friend has gone to live in another part of the country.
- How much would it cost to send a letter to them?
- How much would this cost in a year if you sent a letter every month?

- What if your friend went to live in France?
- What if your friend went to live in the United States of America?

3a Workout

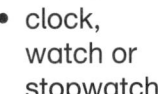
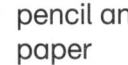

• clock, watch or stopwatch
• pencil and paper

- Design a five-minute workout.

- Think about:
  - how many different exercises you are going to have
  - how long each exercise will take.
- Write down your plan so that someone else could read it and do your five-minute workout.

3b In a minute

• stopwatch
• measuring equipment
• pencil and paper

- How many times can you jump up and down in 10 seconds?
- Use this to work out how many times you would be able to jump up and down in 1 minute.
- What about in 10 minutes? Do you think your answer will be accurate? Why? Why not?

- How long does it take you to run 100 metres?
- Use this to work out how far you could run in 1 minute.
- What about in 10 minutes? Do you think your answer will be accurate? Why? Why not?

3c How fit?

- stopwatch
- skipping rope
- pencil and paper

- Skip for 1 minute.
- Rest.
- Run on the spot for 1 minute.
- Which makes you more out of breath?
- How can you measure this?
- How quickly are you breathing?
- How fast is your heart beating?

- How does this compare with other children in your class?

3d An hour a day

- pencil and paper

'A report from England's chief medical officer says children should aim for 60 minutes of exercise each day.'

- Work out how much exercise you do each day.
- Is this more or less than is recommended? How much more or less?
- If you exercise less than is recommended, what could you do to increase the amount of exercise you do each day?

- Think about all the different types of exercise you do each day.
- Don't forget about walking fast and walking up and down stairs.
- Don't forget about the exercise you get in the playground.

4a Investigating tangrams

- tangram
- pencil and paper

The tangram was invented in China more than 4000 years ago. According to legend, a man called Tan was taking a ceramic tile to the Emperor when he slipped and dropped it. The tile broke into seven pieces. While he was trying to put the tile back together, he found he could make many different figures and designs.

- Look at the seven shapes that make up a tangram.
  Write about the different shapes and sizes. What relationships can you see between the different shapes and sizes?

4b Tangram shapes

- a friend
- 2 tangrams

- Choose a friend.
- Use your tangram to make a shape.
- Show your shape to your friend and ask them to make it using their tangram.

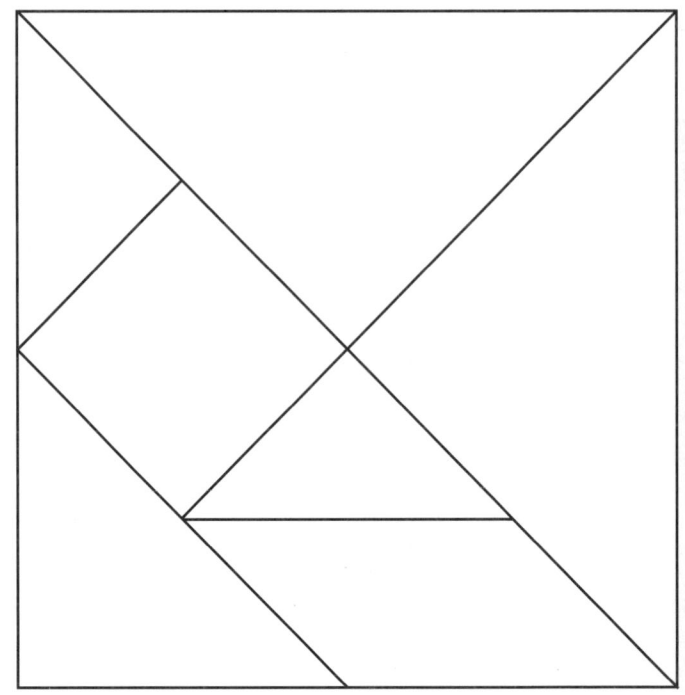

- What shapes can you make using two tangrams?

Tangram animals

• tangram
• pencil and paper

- Use all the pieces of your tangram to make a fox.
- Can you make a dog?
- What about a rabbit?

- What other animals can you make?
- Can you make other pictures?

Design your own tangram

• ruler
• scissors
• pencil and paper

How to make a tangram.
- *Draw a square.*
- *Mark the half-way points A, B, C and D.*
- *Mark the quarter-way point E.*
- *Use these as guides to draw the lines on the square.*

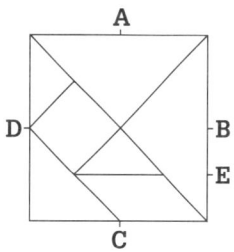
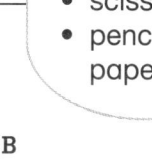

- Design your own tangram.
- What shapes can you make?
- How does your tangram compare with an ordinary 7-piece tangram? Is it as good? Why? Why not?

- Think about:
  - the shape you are going to use to make your tangram
  - the different shapes that will make up your tangram
  - the number of pieces your tangram will have.

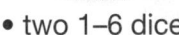

5a

2 dice totals

3 dots and 6 dots.
That's a total of 9 dots.

- two 1–6 dice
- two 0–9 dice
- two 1–12 dice
- two 1–20 dice
- pencil and paper

- Roll two 1–6 dice.
- Count the total number of dots on the top of both dice.
- Write this down.
- Do this 20 times.
- What is the most common total? Why do you think this is so?
- Now do the same thing using two 0–9 dice.
- What is the most common total? Why do you think this is so?

- Predict then test what you think would be the most common total using two 1–12 dice.
- What if you used two 1–20 dice?

5b

Greatest total

- three 1–6 dice
- pencil and paper

- Roll three 1–6 dice.
- What is the greatest total you can get using the numbers of dots on the dice and any of the four operations?

- Think about:
  – which operations you will use
  – if you will use the same or different operations.

Dice

5c Total dots

- six 1–6 dice
- pencil and paper

- Using four 1–6 dice, place them side by side to make a wall.

- Without looking, work out how many spots there are on the bottom of the wall.

- Without looking, work out how many dots there are altogether where the faces of the four dice touch.

- Can you arrange the dice so that there is the same number of spots on the top of the wall as on the bottom of the wall?

- Try using 5 or 6 dice.

Dice

5d Make a die

- card
- ruler
- sticky tape
- glue
- pencil and paper

- Think about the different ways you could make a 1–6 die.
- Which is the best way? Why?
- Make your die.
- On which faces are you going to place the different numbers of dots?

- After you have made your die, write down instructions so a friend could make the same die in the same way that you made it.

6a Right angle programmes

• television guide
• pencil and paper

- Look at a television guide.
- Choose a channel.
- Investigate how many right angles the minute hand turns through for the different programmes during the day.

- Looking at all the channels on one day, during which programme does the minute hand turn through the most right angles?
- What about the least right angles?

6b How much television?

• television guide
• pencil and paper

- On which day of the week do you watch the most television?
- How much is this?
- What fraction is this of all the television you watch during the week?

- For each day of the week, what fraction of your waking time do you spend watching television?

6c Favourite programme

- television guide
- pencil and paper

- What is your favourite television programme?
- How does this compare with other children in your class?
- What is the most popular television programme in your class?

- What do you think is the most popular television programme in your school? How are you going to find out?

6d Pay TV

- television guide
- pencil and paper

- You pay to go to the cinema, the theatre, a sporting event or a concert, but what if you had to pay to watch each television programme?
- What would be a fair price for each programme you watch?
- How much money would you spend on television a day? What about a week? Can you work out how much you would spend in a year?

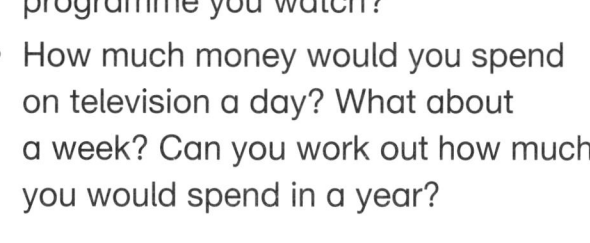

- Think about how much you will charge for different:
  - types of programmes, e.g. news, sports, soaps, cartoons, films …
  - days of the week
  - times of the day.

7a Pattern code

The secret code to open the safe is 3, 8, 6, 4, 3, 8.

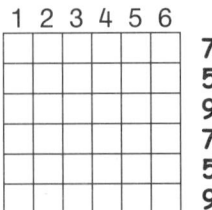

- pencil and paper

	1	2	3	4	5	6	
			▓				3
		▓		▓	▓		8
			▓		▓		6
	▓			▓			4
			▓				3
	▓				▓		8

- Design a pattern where the secret code is 7, 5, 9, 7, 5, 9.
- Is there more than one way of making a pattern for this code?

	1	2	3	4	5	6	
							7
							5
							9
							7
							5
							9

- Design a code and pattern for a friend to solve.

7b Wheel code

- scissors
- pencil and paper

- Cut out the two circles.
- Use them to make your own secret code.
- Write a message for a friend in your secret code and give it to them to solve.

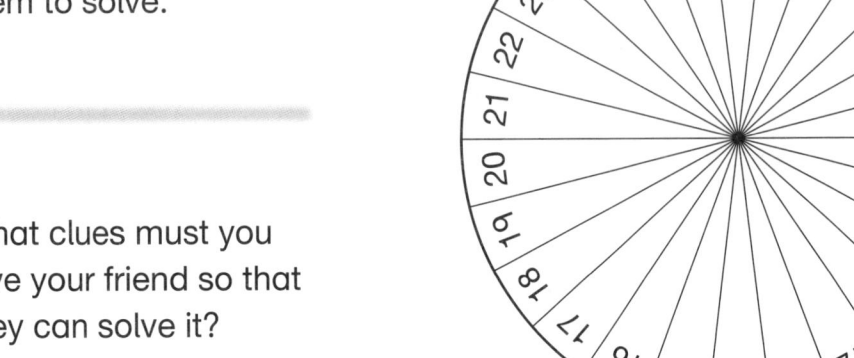

- What clues must you give your friend so that they can solve it?

7c Binary code

• pencil and paper

The Binary code is a way of writing any number using only zeros and ones. It is the system that all computers use.

$I I O I O = (1 \times 16) + (1 \times 8) + (0 \times 4) + (1 \times 2) + (0 \times 1) = 26$

512	256	128	64	32	16	8	4	2	1
					I	I	O	I	O

NOTE: You only fill in the squares up to the largest number that you need. You don't put anything to the left of the largest number.

$I O O O I O O I O I = 512 + 32 + 4 + 1 = 549$

512	256	128	64	32	16	8	4	2	1
I	O	O	O	I	O	O	I	O	I

• Choose ten 2-digit numbers and write them in the binary code.

• Choose ten 3-digit numbers and write them in the binary code.

7d Make your own code

• pencil and paper

• Make a code of your own.
• Your code must include numbers.
• The code must be used to decipher word messages.
• Write out the following message using your code:

WHEN SPIES USE BUGS AND CODES

FOR SOLVING MYSTERIES,

THEY JAIL VILLAINS QUICKLY.

• When you have written the message above in your code, use the same code to write out your own secret message underneath. Give it to a friend to solve.

8a

Planning a school menu

- Plan a healthy and appetising school menu for a week.
- Remember to give some choice in your menu.

- How much will you charge for each item?
- Does it offer value for money?

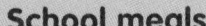

8b

Left over food

- measuring equipment
- pencil and paper

- What is the weight of food left over after school dinner each day?
- How much is this in a week?
- How could this be reduced?

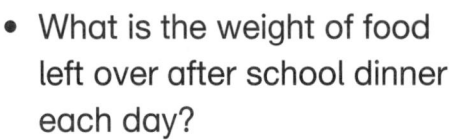

- Does the amount of left over food have anything to do with what's on the menu for that day? Investigate.
- Does it depend on how many options there are on the menu that day?

8c Value for money

- Investigate the cost of school dinners against the cost of packed lunches.
- Which provides the best value for money? Why?

- Think about the cost of an average:
  – school dinner
  – packed lunch.

8d Popular dinners

- How many children in your class ate school dinners yesterday?
- What was the most popular dinner?

- How many children in your class brought packed lunches to school yesterday?
- Was there anything in common about what was in the packed lunches?

9a School road

* pencil and paper

* Investigate the road that your school is on.

* On average, how many vehicles travel on the road each hour / each day?

* When is the road busier / quieter throughout the day / week?

* What fraction of the vehicles are cars / lorries / motorcycles / bicycles etc?

* Is there any provision for people crossing the road? How long do people have to wait to cross the road? Does this differ at different times of the day? Is there a need for a pedestrian crossing or lights?

* How does this road compare with the High Street / the street in which you live?

9b Traffic lights

* watch or stopwatch
* pencil and paper

* Investigate the nearest set of traffic lights to your school.

* How long do the lights remain green / orange / red on each road?

* How long is the green, orange, red sequence on each road?

* Does one road have priority over another road? Why?

* Why are lights needed here?

* Do pedestrians ever have priority? How often? For how long?

9c   Public transport

• public transport timetables
• pencil and paper

- Investigate the public transport in your area.

- Think about:
  - what types of public transport there are
  - where you can travel to
  - how often each type of transport runs
  - if there is enough of each type
  - how punctual each type of transport is
  - how much each type of transport costs.

9d   Cost of public transport

• pencil and paper

- Plan a trip by public transport to a place you would like to visit.
- Find out how much this will cost you.

- Think about:
  - how you will get there, by train, bus, coach …
  - when you are going to travel, what time of the day and which day of the week. Will this make a difference to the cost?
  - who you will take with you. Don't forget to allow for their fares as well. Will their fare be the same as yours?

10a Happy Birthday Daphne

31st December 2004

Happy 97th Birthday Daphne Herne

With love from your daughters, Lorna (77), Joan (74) and Valda (69), your grandchildren Ray (52), Wayne (50), Johnny (49), Jimmy (44), Marella (39) and Peter (37), your great-grandchildren Alan (30), Daniel (28), Michael (23), Darren (22), Justin (22), Aaron, (21), Allison (19), Christopher (17), Jessie (17), Blaze (12), Craig (10) and great-great-grandchild Taylah (1).

- In what years were Daphne and all her descendants born?

- Draw a family tree for Daphne Herne and her family.

10b Living relations

- How many living relations do you have?
- When were they born?
- How old is everyone?
- Draw your family tree.

- Who in your class has the most living relations?

Relations

10c Could your relations …?

• pencil and paper

• Could your great-grandfather have travelled on the Titanic?

• Who in your family could have watched the first moon landing?

Relations

10d Brothers and sisters

• ruler
• pencil and paper

• How many brothers and sisters do each of the children in your class have?
• Draw a graph to show your results.
• What is the most common number?
• Now find out how many brothers and sisters the parents of the children in your class have.
• Draw a graph showing these results.
• What is the most common number?

• What about your grandparents?

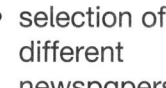

11a How many papers?

- Visit your local newsagents and find out how many copies of each newspaper they sell each day.
- Draw a graph to show your results.

- Using the information you have found out and the prices of the different newspapers, work out how much money the newsagent takes in a day for each newspaper title.
- Now draw another graph showing these results.
- Compare the two graphs. Write about what you notice.

11b Fractions of a newspaper

- Choose a newspaper and investigate what fractions of its pages are about different topics, e.g. news, current affairs, sports, entertainment …

- Do the same thing for a different newspaper. Compare your results.

11c Numbers in papers

- selection of different newspapers
- pencil and paper

- Choose a newspaper.
- Start at the beginning and write down all the numbers you notice. Be sure to include any word or symbol that the number refers to.
- Make two lists – those where you understand how the numbers have been used, and those where you don't.
- Choose two of the things from the list that you don't understand and find out what they mean.

- Ask a friend to help you.
- What else can you use to find out the meanings?

11d The value of newspapers

- selection of different newspapers
- measuring equipment
- pencil and paper

- Is there a relationship between the weight of different newspapers and how much they cost?
- Is this a good way of deciding whether or not a newspaper is good value for money?

- What other ways could you use to judge whether a newspaper is good value for money or not? Are these better ways? Why? Why not?

12a Clothing weights

- measuring equipment
- pencil and paper

- What is the weight of the clothes you wear? (Don't forget your shoes!)

- How is this different at different times of the year?
- How is this different when you are doing different things?

12b Tailor made

- measuring equipment
- pencil and paper

- A tailor is going to make some clothes especially for you.
- Draw a simple figure of yourself.
- Ask a friend to measure you and write the measurements on the figure you have drawn.

- Think about:
  - the type of clothes you would like
  - what measurements the tailor will need to make them, e.g. size of your waist, the length of your arms and legs…

12c Clothe yourself

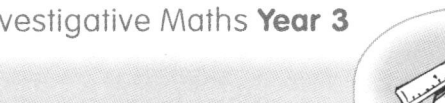

• clothing catalogues
• pencil and paper

- Look through the pages of a clothing catalogue.
- Choose a complete new outfit for yourself.
- How much will this cost you?

- Imagine you are going away for half-term. Where are you going? Choose the clothing you want to take with you. Make sure it's appropriate for where you're going.
- How much will this cost altogether? Remember, you have to be able to carry it all!

12d New school uniform

• pencil and paper

- Your school is getting a new uniform.
- How many pieces of each type of clothing will your school need to order?

- Think about:
  - the different types of clothing needed for boys and girls
  - a summer uniform
  - a winter uniform
  - how many pieces of each type of clothing each child in the school will need.

13 Odd and even 3-digit numbers

- 1–9 digit cards
- pencil and paper

- Shuffle a set of 1–9 digit cards.
- Deal the top three cards and place them face up on the table.

3 7 2

- Use these cards to make six different 3-digit numbers.
- Write the numbers in two lists: odd and even.
- How many odd / even numbers do you have?
- Explain why there is a different number of each.
- Choose another three cards so that you can make more even numbers than odd numbers.
- Choose another three cards so that you can make more odd numbers than even numbers.
- Is it possible to choose three cards so that the number of even numbers and odd numbers is the same? Why?

- What if you dealt four cards and used them to make 24 different 4-digit numbers?

---

14 Number sequences

- pencil and paper

Lucky dip

- Choose one of the numbers above.
- Write a sequence that has your number as its middle number.
- Choose another number and do the same thing.
- Now choose any two numbers and write a sequence that has your numbers as the end two numbers.

- Choose any three numbers and write a sequence that has your numbers in it.

15 Seeing patterns

- Choose a number from 1 to 10.
- Starting with this number, count on in 5s.
- Create a number sequence of at least 10 numbers.
- What patterns do you notice?
- Choose a different start number and do this again. Do you always see the same patterns?

- pencil and paper

- What if you counted on in 3s, 4s, 6s, 7s, 8s or 9s from a 1-digit number? What patterns do you notice?
- What if you started with a 2-digit number? Do you see the same patterns?

---

16 Numbers between…

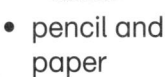

- pencil and paper

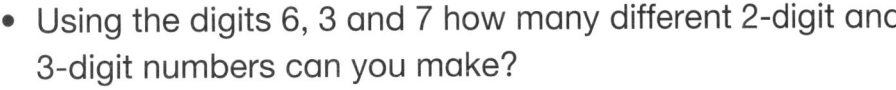

- Using the digits 6, 3 and 7 how many different 2-digit and 3-digit numbers can you make?
- Write the numbers in order, smallest to largest.
- How many numbers between 60 and 600 can you make with these three digits? What are they?

- What if the digits were 2, 5, 7 and 1? How many different 2-digit, 3-digit and 4-digit numbers can you make?

17

1, 10 and 100

- 0–9 die
- pencil and paper

- Roll a 0–9 die three times and write down the numbers.
- Use the three numbers to make as many different 2-digit and 3-digit numbers as you can.
- What is 1, 10 and 100 more than your numbers?
- Write about any patterns you notice.
- Roll the die again and repeat.

- Roll the die four times to make as many different 2-digit, 3-digit and 4-digit numbers as you can. What is 1, 10 and 100 more than your numbers? What patterns do you notice?
- What about 1, 10 and 100 less than your numbers?

18

Rounding

- pencil and paper

- What are all the whole numbers that become 360 when rounded to the nearest 10?

- Investigate other 3-digit multiples of 10.
- What are the whole numbers that become 300 when rounded to the nearest 100?

19 Pages, lines and words

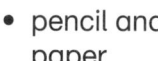
- book
- pencil and paper

- Choose a book from the class library.
- Without opening the book, estimate how many pages it has.
- Open the book to the back page and see how close your estimate was.
- Now open the book to any page. Estimate and then find out how many lines there are on the page.
- Estimate then find out how many words there are on the page.

- Can you estimate how many lines there are in the whole book?
- What about how many words there are?
- Is this approximately the same for other books in your class library?

---

20 Fractions that total 1

- pencil and paper

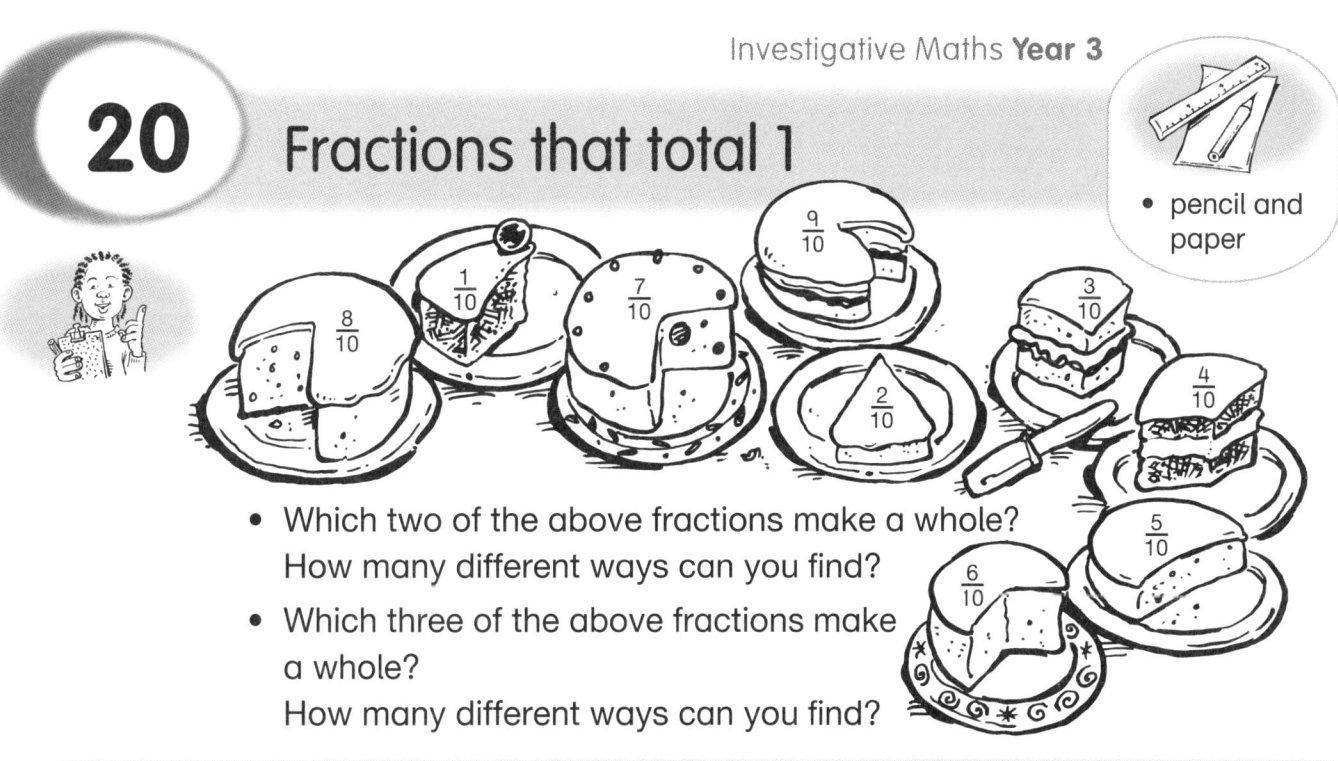

- Which two of the above fractions make a whole?
  How many different ways can you find?
- Which three of the above fractions make a whole?
  How many different ways can you find?

- Which two of the above fractions make a half?
  How many different ways can you find?
- Can you think of other pairs of fractions that make a whole?
  What about a half?

21 Buying sweets

• pencil and paper

- Two children have bought eight sweets between them.
- Investigate what fraction of the eight sweets each child could have bought.

- What if three children buy 12 sweets between them? What fraction could each have bought?
- What about four children buying 10 sweets?

22 Equivalent fractions

• 1–9 digit cards
• pencil and paper

$$\frac{1}{2} = \frac{3}{6}$$

- Lay out four 1–9 digit cards as above to make an equivalent statement.
- How many equivalent statements can you make using four cards from a set of 1–9 digit cards?

- What if you had two sets of 1–9 digit cards and could use the same number twice?

23 Fractions of numbers

- pencil and paper

> 9 is three-quarters of 12.

- Is Robbie right?
- Find pairs of numbers where one number is three-quarters of the other.
- What do you notice about the pairs of numbers?

- Find pairs of numbers where one number is two-thirds of the other.
- What about three-fifths / four-fifths / seven-tenths?

---

24 60 and 100

- 1–9 digit cards
- pencil and paper

- Shuffle a set of 1–9 digit cards, deal the top four cards and place them face up on the table.
- Use the cards to make two 2-digit numbers.
- Add the two numbers together.
- Using the same four digits, make another pair of 2-digit numbers.
- Add these two numbers together.
- Do this three more times.
- Which of your calculations has an answer nearest to 60?
- Which of your calculations has an answer nearest to 100?

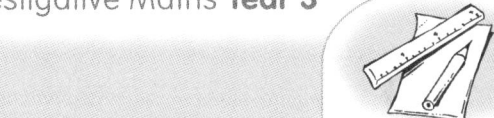

- Can you choose four digit cards to make a calculation with an answer of 80? How many different ways can you do this?
- What about with an answer of 100?

• pencil and paper

25 Pairs of 2-digit numbers

- Choose four of the numbers above to make a pair of 2-digit numbers.
- Add the numbers together.
- Do this 10 times.
- Can you find two different pairs of numbers with the same answer?

- Using only the six numbers above, can you find a pair of 2-digit numbers with a total of 100? How many different pairs can you find?

• pencil and paper

26 Multiples of 10

- Investigate finding three different multiples of 10 with a total of 100.
- Investigate finding four different multiples of 10 with a total of 100.
- What about finding five different multiples of 10 with a total of 100?

- What if you could use the same multiples of 10 more than once, e.g. 20 + 20 + 60?
- What if the numbers were multiples of 100 with a total of 1000?

27 Smaller from the larger

- 0–9 die
- pencil and paper

- Roll a 0–9 die five times and write down the numbers.
- Use four of the numbers rolled to make two 2-digit numbers.
- Subtract the smaller number from the larger number.
- Make as many different subtraction calculations as you can using the five numbers rolled.

- Can you find two different pairs of numbers with the same answer?
- What if you used the five numbers rolled to make a 3-digit number and a 2-digit number, e.g. 291 and 57?

28 Calendar calculations

- calendar
- pencil and paper

- Pick a month on the calendar and choose a 2 × 2 square.
- Add opposite numbers, e.g.
  $10 + 18 = ?$
  $11 + 17 = ?$
- Choose other 2 × 2 squares and do the same.
- What do you notice about your answers?

JANUARY

M	T	W	T	F	S	S
1	2	3	4	5	6	7
8	9	10	11	12	13	14
15	16	17	18	19	20	21
22	23	24	25	26	27	28
29	30	31				

- What do you notice when you find the difference between opposite numbers in 2 × 2 squares?
- Does this work for other months?

29 Choose 3 numbers

• pencil and paper

25.7.18.9.11.26.17.8

I can make 25 different addition and subtraction calculations, with their answers, using 3 of the numbers above in each calculation.

11 + 7 = 18
17 + 8 = 25
25 − 8 = 17

- Is Brian right?

- What if you replaced the number 8 with the number 10 and the number 25 with the number 28?

✂

30 Making numbers

• pencil and paper

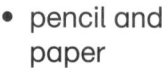

- Using pairs of the numbers on the table, can you add the numbers or find the difference between them to make the numbers below the table?

- Did you use all the numbers?

- What other numbers can you make by adding or subtracting pairs of numbers on the table?

- What about adding or subtracting pairs of numbers under the table?

31   10 card calculations

- 0–9 digit cards
- pencil and paper

- Use a set of 0–9 digit cards to make five addition calculations, all with different answers. Can you find different ways of doing this?

- Now use the cards to make five addition calculations, all with the same answers. Can you find different ways of doing this?

- What if you used the numbers to make subtraction calculations?

© HarperCollins*Publishers* Ltd 2005

---

32   All 2s and 5s

- pencil and paper

- Use only the digits 2, 2, 2, 5, 5, 5 to write addition calculations of two or three 2-digit numbers, e.g. 22 + 25 = ?

         22 + 25 + 55 = ?

- Work out the answers to your calculations.

- What if you used the digits to make subtraction calculations of two 2-digit numbers, e.g. 52 – 25 = ?

- What if you used the digits to make calculations of three 2-digit numbers, e.g. 25 + 55 – 52 = ?

- What about using the digits to make calculations involving two 3-digit numbers?

© HarperCollins*Publishers* Ltd 2005

• pencil and paper

33 409

• Investigate addition calculations of 3-digit and 2-digit numbers that have the answer 409.

• What if 2-digit numbers were subtracted from 3-digit numbers and the answer was still 409?

• What about calculations involving two 3-digit numbers?

• What about having an answer of 612?

34 Making palindromic numbers

• 1–9 digit cards
• pencil and paper

The digits in a palindromic number read the same backwards as forwards.

121 737 55 666 343 575

• Use four 1–9 digit cards to make two 2-digit numbers.

• Add the numbers together.

• How many answers can you find that are palindromic numbers?

• What if you used four of the digit cards to make two 2-digit numbers and found the difference between the two numbers? How many answers could you find that are palindromic numbers?

• pencil and paper

35 Date of birth

I was born on 27 / 05 / 1997.
The 8 digits that make up my date
of birth are: 2, 7, 0, 5, 1, 9, 9, 7.

• Write down the eight digits that make up your date of birth.
• Choose any six of these digits to make two 3-digit numbers.
• Add the two numbers together and write down the answer.
• What's the largest number you can make by choosing any six of your eight digits and repeating as above?

• Repeat as above but subtract the smaller 3-digit number from the larger.
• What's the smallest answer you can make?
• What's the nearest answer to 800 you can make by either adding or subtracting the numbers?

• pencil and paper

36 Odd and even calculations

If you subtract a pair of odd
numbers, the answer is even.

• Is Caroline right?
• Can you find two odd numbers that have a difference that is an odd number?

If you add two odd numbers
together the answer is also even.

• Is Caroline right this time?
• What if you found the difference between two even numbers? What about adding two even numbers?
• What about an odd number and an even number?

37 Which signs?

• pencil and paper

- Write an addition or subtraction sign in each of the boxes to make the calculations true.

3 ☐ 6 ☐ 8 ☐ 5 ☐ 4 = 8

3 ☐ 6 ☐ 8 ☐ 5 ☐ 4 = 2

10 ☐ 2 ☐ 9 ☐ 2 ☐ 1 = 16

5 ☐ 1 ☐ 4 ☐ 5 ☐ 4 = 1

7 ☐ 2 ☐ 8 ☐ 4 ☐ 5 = 0

- Make some problems like these for your friends to solve.

---

38 Multiplying by 10 and 100

• 0–9 die
• pencil and paper

- Roll a 0–9 die twice.
- Use the two numbers rolled to make a 2-digit number.
- Multiply the number by 10, and by 100.
- Write down your answers.
- Do this 10 times.
- What do you notice?

- What if you rolled the die three times to make a 3-digit number?

39 Double multiplications

• pencil and paper

• Start with a multiplication calculation.
• Double each number to make a new calculation.
• Keep doing this for as long as you can.
• What do you notice about each of your answers?
• Does this always work?

$4 \times 2 = 8$
$8 \times 4 = 32$
$16 \times 8 =$

• What if you only double the first number?
• What if you only double the second number?
• What do you notice?

40 Halving chains

• pencil and paper

This is a 3-link chain.

• Choose a 2-digit even number and keep halving until you reach an odd number.
• What is the longest chain you can make starting with a 2-digit number?

• What if you started with a 3-digit number?

41 Dividing by 10 and 100

- pencil and paper

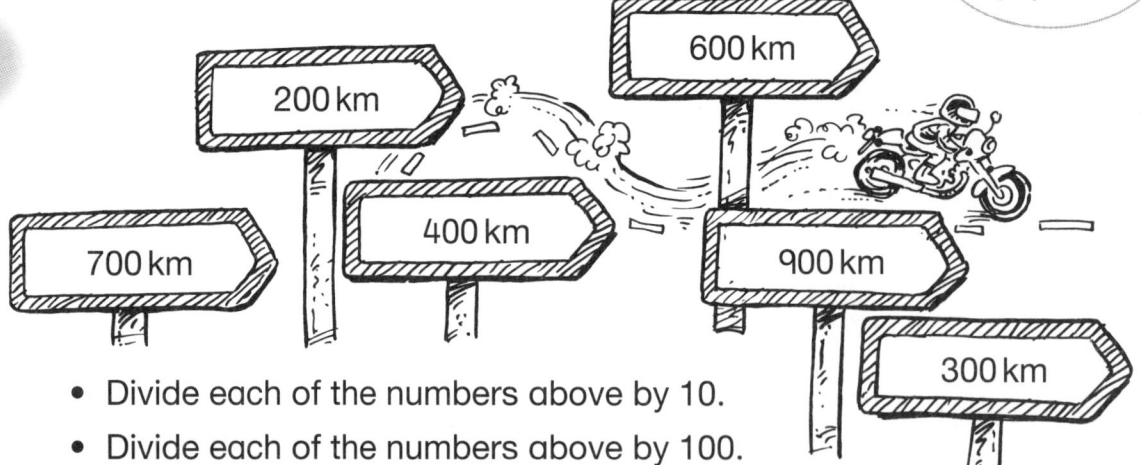

- Divide each of the numbers above by 10.
- Divide each of the numbers above by 100.
- What do you notice about your answers?

- Choose some numbers of your own and divide each of them by 10.
- Can you also divide them by 100?

42 Remainder of 1

- bag with 1–9 digit cards inside
- pencil and paper

- Pick three digit cards from the bag.
- Arrange them to make a 2-digit number and a 1-digit number.
- Divide the 2-digit number by the 1-digit number.
- Investigate what division calculations you can make that have answers with a remainder of 1.
- Choose another three cards and repeat as above.

- What about calculations with a remainder of 2, 3, 4...8, 9?

43 More remainders

• pencil and paper

- Write down ten 2-digit numbers.
- Divide each of your numbers by 3.
- Which numbers have no remainder?
- Which numbers have a remainder of 1 / 2?
- Write about any patterns you notice.

- Divide different 2-digit numbers by 4, and sort them according to their remainders.
- Do you notice any patterns?
- What if you divide by 5 or 6?

44 Special squares

• pencil and paper

- The squares below are special. If you multiply diagonally the answers are the same.

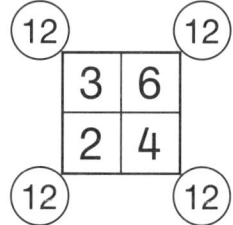 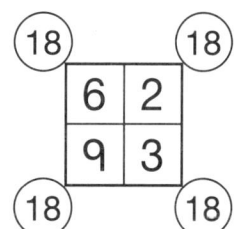

- Can you make some special squares of your own?

- What if you had a mixture of 1-digit and 2-digit numbers in the boxes?
- Can you make special squares where if you divide diagonally the answers are the same?

- pencil and paper

45 Multiplications and divisions

2 3 4 5 6 12 15 18 20 24 30 × =

$3 \times 4 = 12$
$4 \times 3 = 12$
$12 \times 2 = 24$

- Use only the numbers and signs above to make as many calculations as you can.

- What if you replaced $\times$ with $\div$?

- pencil and paper

46 × ÷ 10 100

- Choose four of the following cards to make a correct number sentence.

6 60 600 6000 =

×10 ×100 ÷10 ÷100

- How many different number sentences can you make by arranging the cards?
- Write about what you notice.

- What if you used these number cards instead?  7 70 700 7000

47 Making 24

- Using two or more of the numbers in the points of the star make a calculation with an answer of 24.
- How many different ways can you find?

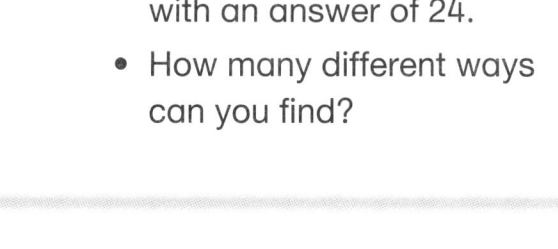

- Choose your own six numbers to go in the points of the star. Use them to make calculations with an answer of 36.

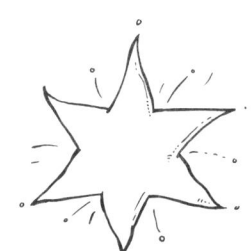

- What about if you also chose the answer to make?

48 Toy cars

TOY CARS
Prices range from £1.20 to £3.80.

- At the toyshop, the cost of four cars is £10.60. What could be the price of each car?

- If the two fastest cars cost £3.80 each, what could the other two cars cost?

• pencil and paper

49 1 note and 3 coins

- In your purse you have one note and three identical coins.
- Investigate how much money could be in your purse.

- What if you had one coin and three identical notes in your purse?

• pencil and paper

50 Receiving change

- Investigate what amounts you could spend using £1 for which you would receive only one coin in change.

- What about if you received two coins in change?

51 Measuring with ropes

• pencil and paper

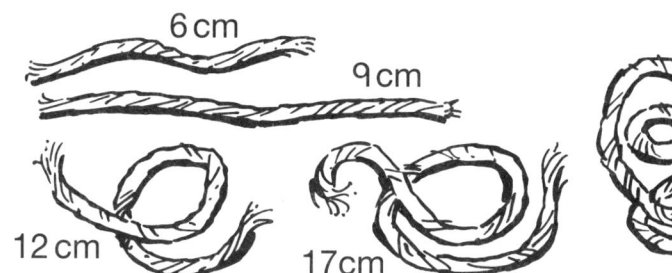

6 cm

9 cm

21cm

12 cm

17cm

• Using only the ropes above, which lengths can you measure from 1 cm to 30 cm?

• You can place ropes end to end to find the total length, or side by side to find the difference.

• Which lengths can you not measure?

• Which five different lengths of rope would you need to have to make every length from 1 cm to 30 cm?

---

52 50 g, 100 g and 500 g

• pencil and paper

• Using the weights above, investigate using them to balance objects with a mass of 50 g, 100 g, 150 g, 200 g… up to 500 g.

• You must use the fewest number of weights each time.

• Could you use the weights to balance objects with a mass 550 g, 600 g, 650 g, 700 g … up to 1 kg?

• What if you only had one of each different weight? Which objects could you balance? Which would be impossible?

53 Filling buckets

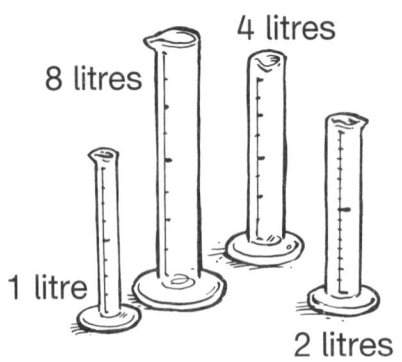

8 litres

4 litres

1 litre

2 litres

- How can you fill buckets from 1 litre to 30 litres using only the measuring cylinders above?
- The measuring cylinders must be full and you must fill them as few times as possible.

- What if you have measuring cylinders of $\frac{1}{4}$ litre, $\frac{1}{2}$ litre, 1 litre, 3 litres and 8 litres? How many different amounts could you measure if you can only fill each container once?

---

54 This year

- Without using a calendar, work out for this year, what day of the week is:
  - 8th February
  - 1st April
  - 14th July
  - 29th September
  - 11th November.

- This year, what date is:
  - the first Saturday in January
  - the third Wednesday in May
  - the last Tuesday in June
  - the first Monday in August
  - the second Sunday in December?

55 Weekend

• How many Saturdays and Sundays are there altogether this year?

• Which day of the week is there the most of this year?

---

56 Decking

• Imagine 36 one-metre square blocks of decking.
• Investigate the possible sizes of rectangular patio you could build using them all.

• What if you had another 12 one-metre square blocks?

57 Symmetrical flags

- Using the flag on the right as a model, make as many different flags as possible using no more than two colours.
- Each square must be all one colour.
- How many vertical or horizontal lines of symmetry does each flag have?

- 2 coloured pencils
- ruler
- mirror
- pencil and paper

- What if you coloured this flag using no more than 2 colours?

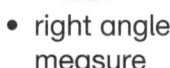

58 Right angle shapes

This pentagon has two right angles.

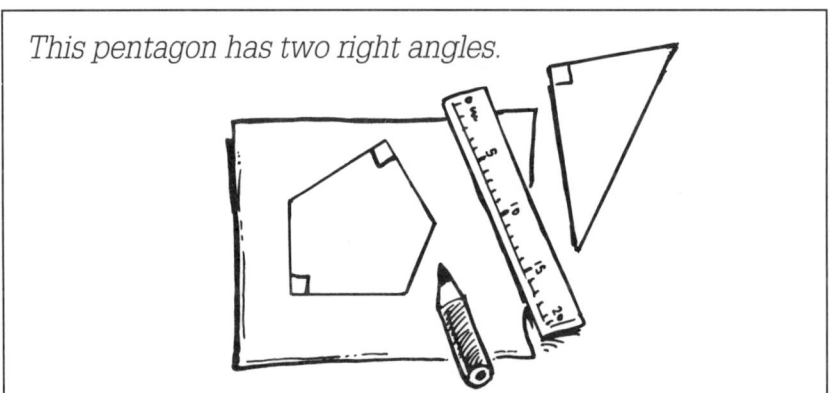

- right angle measure
- ruler
- pencil and paper

- What other pentagons can you draw that have two right angles?
- Can you draw other pentagons that have more than two right angles?

- Can you draw a hexagon with two right angles? What about more than two right angles?
- What about octagons?

• pencil and paper

59 Ronnie the Robot

I programmed Ronnie to get home by walking forward 4 paces, turning left 90°, walking forward 4 paces, turning left 90° and walking forward 2 paces.

- Is Annie right?
- What is the shortest route you could programme Ronnie to walk from work to home?

- What if Ronnie had to stop off at Robotic Mechanics  and then at The Fuel Stop on his way home?

• set of 2D shapes
• pencil and paper

60 Tessellating shapes

A tessellation is a pattern made by repeating the same 2D shape over and over again.

- Investigate which regular 2D shapes tessellate.

- Can you make a tessellation from two or more different regular 2D shapes?

Answers

Activity 13

When three digit cards are used to make six different 3-digit numbers there will never be the same number of odd and even numbers. If, for example, three even digits are chosen, say 2, 4 and 6, there will be six even numbers and no odd numbers. Likewise, if three odd digits are chosen, say 1, 3 and 7, there will be six odd numbers and no even numbers. Also, if there are two odd digits and one even digit, (or two even digits and one odd digit) there will always be more odd numbers (or even numbers).

Activity 15

When counting on in 5s from any single-digit number, e.g. 4, there is a repeating pattern of the units digits alternating between the single-digit number you started with, i.e. 4 and the number that is 5 more than this, i.e. 9. A pattern also occurs in that there are only ever two numbers in each decade, i.e. two 'teens' numbers, two '20s' numbers, two '30s' numbers and so on.

Activity 16

12 different 2-digit and 3-digit numbers can be made using the digits 6, 3 and 7:
36, 37, 63, 67, 73, 76, 367, 376, 637, 673, 736 and 763.

6 numbers lie between 60 and 600, they are: 63, 67, 73, 76, 367 and 376.

Activity 18

355, 356, 357, 358, 359, 361, 362, 363, 364.

Activity 20

There are 4 different ways to use 2 fractions to make a whole:

$\frac{1}{10} + \frac{9}{10}$

$\frac{2}{10} + \frac{8}{10}$

$\frac{3}{10} + \frac{7}{10}$

$\frac{4}{10} + \frac{6}{10}$

There are 4 different ways to use 3 fractions to make a whole:

$\frac{7}{10} + \frac{2}{10} + \frac{1}{10}$

$\frac{6}{10} + \frac{3}{10} + \frac{1}{10}$

$\frac{5}{10} + \frac{4}{10} + \frac{1}{10}$

$\frac{5}{10} + \frac{3}{10} + \frac{2}{10}$

Activity 21

Child A could have bought $\frac{1}{8}$ of the sweets and Child B $\frac{7}{8}$, and vice versa.

Child A could have bought $\frac{1}{4}$ of the sweets and Child B $\frac{3}{4}$, and vice versa.

Child A could have bought $\frac{3}{8}$ of the sweets and Child B $\frac{5}{8}$, and vice versa.

Child A and Child B could each have bought $\frac{1}{2}$ of the sweets.

Activity 22

You can make 10 equivalent statements using one set of 1–9 digit cards.

$\frac{1}{2} = \frac{3}{6}$ $\frac{1}{2} = \frac{4}{8}$

$\frac{3}{6} = \frac{4}{8}$ $\frac{2}{4} = \frac{3}{6}$

$\frac{1}{3} = \frac{2}{6}$ $\frac{2}{6} = \frac{3}{9}$

$\frac{2}{3} = \frac{4}{6}$ $\frac{2}{3} = \frac{6}{9}$

$\frac{1}{4} = \frac{2}{8}$ $\frac{3}{4} = \frac{6}{8}$

Activity 23

Pairs of numbers where one number is three-quarters of the other may include:
– 3 and 4
– 6 and 8
– 12 and 16
– 15 and 20
Other pairs are possible.

The first numbers are all multiples of 3, the second all multiples of 4.

Activity 26

3 different multiples of 10 with a total of 100 are:

10 + 20 + 70   10 + 30 + 60

10 + 40 + 50   20 + 30 + 50

4 different multiples of 10 with a total of 100 are:

10 + 20 + 30 + 40

It is impossible to have 5 different multiples of 10 with a total of 100.

Activity 28

Opposite totals are equal.

Activity 29

Brian is not right. There are 24 different addition and subtraction calculations that can be made using these numbers, if children do not apply the commutative law, or 18 if they do.

11 + 7 = 18	8 + 9 = 17
7 + 11 = 18	9 + 8 = 17
18 – 7 = 11	17 – 9 = 8
18 – 11 = 7	17 – 8 = 9

18 + 7 = 25	17 + 8 = 25
7 + 18 = 25	8 + 17 = 25
25 – 7 = 18	25 – 8 = 17
25 – 18 = 7	25 – 17 = 8

18 + 8 = 26	17 + 9 = 26
8 + 18 = 26	9 + 17 = 26
26 – 8 = 18	26 – 9 = 17
26 – 18 = 8	26 – 17 = 9

Activity 30

39 + 26 = 65	47 – 26 = 21
47 – 39 = 8	39 – 26 = 13
26 + 47 = 73	39 + 47 = 86

You do not use the numbers 12, 14 or 50.

Activity 31

Many answers are possible using all 10 numbers to make five addition calculations all with different answers, e.g.

0 + 5 = 5	1 + 6 = 7
2 + 7 = 9	3 + 8 = 11
4 + 9 = 13	

All 10 numbers can be arranged to make five addition calculations with an answer of 9, i.e.

0 + 9 = 9	1 + 8 = 9
2 + 7 = 9	3 + 6 = 9
4 + 5 = 9	

Activity 32

$22 + 25 = 47$
$22 + 52 = 74$
$25 + 25 = 50$
$25 + 52 = 77$
$52 + 52 = 104$
$55 + 22 = 77$
$55 + 25 = 80$
$55 + 52 = 107$
$22 + 25 + 55 = 102$
$22 + 52 + 55 = 129$
$25 + 25 + 25 = 75$
$52 + 52 + 52 = 156$
$25 + 25 + 52 = 102$
$25 + 52 + 52 = 129$

Activity 33

Any 3-digit number and 2-digit number that total 409, e.g. $356 + 53$

Activity 34

Only the following palindromic totals are possible by adding two 2-digit numbers: 55, 66, 77, 88, 99, 101, 111, 121, 131, 141, 151, 161 and 171.

All 2-digit plus 2-digit calculations that have different digits in each of the 2-digit numbers and total the above numbers are correct, e.g.
$55 = 43 + 12$ $121 = 73 + 48$
$66 = 47 + 19$ $131 = 82 + 49$
$77 = 53 + 24$ $141 = 95 + 46$
$88 = 65 + 23$ $151 = 87 + 64$
$99 = 53 + 46$ $161 = 76 + 85$
$101 = 82 + 19$ $171 = 96 + 75$
$111 = 75 + 36$

Other calculations are possible.

Activity 36

Caroline is right, the difference between a pair of odd numbers is always even.

Activity 37

$3 + 6 + 8 - 5 - 4 = 8$
$3 + 6 - 8 + 5 - 4 = 2$
$10 - 2 + 9 - 2 + 1 = 16$
$5 - 1 - 4 + 5 - 4 = 1$
$7 + 2 - 8 + 4 - 5 = 0$

Activity 38

When multiplying a number by 10 or 100 the digits do not change only their place values change, and the number becomes ten or one hundred times greater.

Activity 39

New answers are four times the previous answer.

Activity 40

A 6-link chain can be made starting with the number 64, (i.e. $64 \rightarrow 32 \rightarrow 16 \rightarrow 8 \rightarrow 4 \rightarrow 2 \rightarrow 1$)

Activity 41

When dividing a number by 10 or 100 the digits do not change only their place values change, and the number becomes ten or one hundred times smaller.

Activity 43

When dividing a number by 3:
– numbers that are multiples of 3 have no remainders
– numbers that are one more than a multiple of 3 have a remainder of 1
– numbers that are two more than a multiple of 3 have a remainder of 2.

Activity 45

$2 \times 3 = 6$ $3 \times 4 = 12$
$3 \times 2 = 6$ $4 \times 3 = 12$
$2 \times 6 = 12$ $3 \times 5 = 15$
$6 \times 2 = 12$ $5 \times 3 = 15$
$2 \times 12 = 24$ $3 \times 6 = 18$
$12 \times 2 = 24$ $6 \times 3 = 18$
$2 \times 15 = 30$
$15 \times 2 = 30$

$4 \times 5 = 20$ $5 \times 6 = 30$
$5 \times 4 = 20$ $6 \times 5 = 30$
$4 \times 6 = 24$
$6 \times 4 = 24$

Activity 46

10 different calculations can be made by arranging the cards.
$6 \times 10 = 60$
$60 \times 10 = 600$
$600 \times 10 = 6000$
$6 \times 100 = 600$
$60 \times 100 = 6000$
$60 \div 10 = 6$
$600 \div 10 = 60$
$6000 \div 10 = 600$
$600 \div 100 = 6$
$6000 \div 100 = 60$

When multiplying a number by 10 or 100 the digits do not change only their place values change, and the number becomes ten or one hundred times greater.

When dividing a number by 10 or 100 the digits do not change only their place values change, and the number becomes ten or one hundred times smaller.

Activity 47

Many answers are possible, e.g.
12×2
$10 + 12 + 2$
$10 + 8 + 6$
$(12 - 8) \times 6$
$12 + 10 + 8 - 6$

Activity 48

Any four amounts from £1.20 to £3.80 that total £10.60, for example,
£1.50 + £1.50 + £3.80 + £3.80 or
£1.80 + £2.20 + £3.00 + £3.60

Activity 49

£5 + 1p + 1p + 1p = £5.03
£5 + 2p + 2p + 2p = £5.06
£5 + 5p + 5p + 5p = £5.15
£5 + 10p + 10p + 10p = £5.30
£5 + 20p + 20p + 20p = £5.60
£5 + 50p + 50p + 50p = £6.50
£5 + £1 + £1 + £1 = £8
£5 + £2 + £2 + £2 = £11

£10 + 1p + 1p + 1p = £10.03
£10 + 2p + 2p + 2p = £10.06
£10 + 5p + 5p + 5p = £10.15
£10 + 10p + 10p + 10p
  = £10.30
£10 + 20p + 20p + 20p
  = £10.60
£10 + 50p + 50p + 50p
  = £11.50
£10 + £1 + £1 + £1 = £13
£10 + £2 + £2 + £2 = £16

£20 + 1p + 1p + 1p = £20.03
£20 + 2p + 2p + 2p = £20.06
£20 + 5p + 5p + 5p = £20.15
£20 + 10p + 10p + 10p
  = £20.30
£20 + 20p + 20p + 20p
  = £20.60
£20 + 50p + 50p + 50p
  = £21.50
£20 + £1 + £1 + £1 = £23
£20 + £2 + £2 + £2 = £26

£50 + 1p + 1p + 1p = £50.03
£50 + 2p + 2p + 2p = £50.06
£50 + 5p + 5p + 5p = £50.15
£50 + 10p + 10p + 10p
  = £50.30
£50 + 20p + 20p + 20p
  = £50.60
£50 + 50p + 50p + 50p
  = £51.50
£50 + £1 + £1 + £1 = £53
£50 + £2 + £2 + £2 = £56

Activity 50

99p (1p change)
98p (2p change)
95p (5p change)
90p (10p change)
80p (20p change)
50p (50p change)

Activity 51

You can measure the following
lengths using two pieces of rope:
1 cm = 12 cm + 6 cm − 17 cm
3 cm = 9 cm − 6 cm
4 cm = 21 cm − 17 cm
5 cm = 17 cm − 12 cm
6 cm = 6 cm
8 cm = 17 cm − 9 cm
9 cm = 9 cm
11 cm = 17 cm − 6 cm
12 cm = 12 cm
15 cm = 9 cm + 6 cm
17 cm = 17 cm
18 cm = 12 cm + 6 cm
21 cm = 21 cm
23 cm = 17 cm + 6 cm
26 cm = 17 cm + 9 cm
27 cm = 21 cm + 6 cm
29 cm = 17 cm + 12 cm
30 cm = 21 cm + 9 cm
Other ways are possible.

You can measure the following
lengths using three or more pieces
of rope:
2 cm = (6 cm + 17 cm) − 21 cm
7 cm = (21 cm + 12 cm)
 − (17 cm + 9 cm)
10 cm = (21 cm − 17 cm)
 + (12 cm − 6 cm)
13 cm = (21 cm + 9 cm) − 17 cm
14 cm = (17 cm + 12 cm)
 − (9 cm + 6 cm)
16 cm = (21 cm + 12 cm) − 17 cm
19 cm = (21 cm + 9 cm + 6 cm)
 − 17 cm
20 cm = (17 cm + 9 cm) − 6 cm
22 cm = (21 cm + 12 cm + 6 cm)
 − 17 cm
24 cm = (21 cm + 12 cm) − 9 cm
25 cm = (21 cm + 12 cm + 9 cm)
 − 17 cm
Other ways are possible.

You cannot measure 28 cm.

Activity 52

50 g = 50 g
100 g = 100 g
150 g = 100 g + 50 g
200 g = 100 g + 100 g
250 g = 100 g + 100g + 50 g
300 g = 100 g + 100g + 100 g
 or 500 g − 100 g − 100 g
350 g = 500 g − 100 g − 50 g
400 g = 500 g − 100 g
450 g = 500 g − 50 g
500 g = 500 g

Activity 53

1 litre = 1 litre
2 litres = 2 litres
3 litres = 2 litres + 1 litre
4 litres = 4 litres
5 litres = 4 litres + 1 litre
6 litres = 4 litres + 2 litres
7 litres = 4 litres + 2 litres + 1 litre
8 litres = 8 litres
9 litres = 8 litres + 1 litre
10 litres = 8 litres + 2 litres
11 litres = 8 litres + 2 litres + 1 litre
12 litres = 8 litres + 4 litres
13 litres = 8 litres + 4 litres + 1 litre
14 litres = 8 litres + 4 litres
 + 2 litres
15 litres = 8 litres + 4 litres
 + 2 litres + 1 litre
16 litres = 8 litres + 8 litres
17 litres = 8 litres + 8 litres + 1 litre
18 litres = 8 litres + 8 litres
 + 2 litres
19 litres = 8 litres + 8 litres
 + 2 litres + 1 litre
20 litres = 8 litres + 8 litres
 + 4 litres
21 litres = 8 litres + 8 litres
 + 4 litres + 1 litre
22 litres = 8 litres + 8 litres
 + 4 litres + 2 litres
23 litres = 8 litres + 8 litres
 + 4 litres + 2 litres + 1 litre
24 litres = 8 litres + 8 litres
 + 8 litres
25 litres = 8 litres + 8 litres
 + 8 litres + 1 litre
26 litres = 8 litres + 8 litres
 + 8 litres + 2 litres
27 litres = 8 litres + 8 litres
 + 8 litres + 2 litres + 1 litre
28 litres = 8 litres + 8 litres
 + 8 litres + 4 litres
29 litres = 8 litres + 8 litres
 + 8 litres + 4 litres + 1 litre
30 litres = 8 litres + 8 litres
 + 8 litres + 4 litres + 2 litres

Activity 56

1 metre × 36 metres
2 metres × 18 metres
3 metres × 12 metres
4 metres × 9 metres

Also allow 6 metres × 6 metres

Activity 57

No lines of symmetry

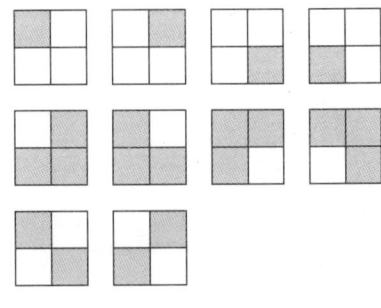

1 line of symmetry

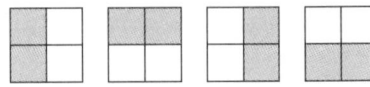

2 lines of symmetry

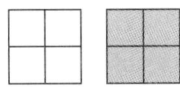

Activity 58

Many different pentagons can
be drawn with one, two or three
right angles. You cannot draw a
pentagon with more than three
right angles.

Activity 59

Annie is not right. Ronnie should
have been programmed to travel
forward 4 paces, turn left 90°,
walk forward 4 paces, turn **right**
90° and walk forward 2 paces.
The shortest route is 10 paces.
Many routes are possible walking
10 paces.

Activity 60

Squares, rectangles, triangles and
hexagons all tessellate.